"I Can Do Anything"

The Sammy Davis, Jr. Story

William Schoell

Avisson Press, Inc
Greensboro

ISBN 1-888105-61-5
First edition
Printed in the USA

Library of Congress Cataloging-in-Publication Data

Schoell. William.
  "I can do anything": the Sammy Davis, Jr. story / William Schoell.—1st ed.
    p.cm. — (Avisson young adult series)
  Summary: Describes the life and career of Sammy Davis, Jr., the African American entertainer and film star.
  Includes bibliographical references and index.
  ISBN 1-888105-61-5 (pbk.)
    1. Davis, Sammy, 1925—Juvenile literature. 2. Entertainers—United States—Biography—Juvenile literature. [1. Davis, Sammy, 1925-
2. Entertainers. 3. African Americans—Biography.] I. Title. II. Series.

PN2287.D322S36 2004
792.7'028'092—dc22
[B]

2003057904

Contents

Chapter One

Vaudeville Days

They called him "Silent Sam, The Dancing Midget."

The little person on stage with the two bigger men was not a midget, however; he was a child of five named Sammy Davis Jr. Sammy had been born in Harlem on December 8th, 1925 to two entertainers named Sammy and Elvera Davis. The black couple traveled the country performing song and dance routines on stage in various vaudeville troupes. Vaudeville was a popular form of entertainment in the days before motion picture screens, and then television sets, completely dominated show business.

Sammy Sr. and his wife, the former chorus girl Elvera "Baby" Sanchez, were both touring in *Holiday in Dixieland* when Sammy was born. Elvera took two weeks off to have the baby, then left little Sammy with friends so she could continue with the tour with her husband.

"I Can Do Anything"

Holiday in Dixieland was a show put together by a man named Will Mastin, who would later play a large role in young Sammy's life as well.

Sammy Senior and Elvera broke up not long after Sammy was born. Seeking greener pastures, Elvera joined another vaudeville troupe and left her baby with his father. Things proceeded on a downward course for Sammy Sr.. *Holiday in Dixieland* eventually used up its bookings, and the elder Davis attached himself to other traveling shows. Wherever he went he took little Sammy with him.

Things were okay for awhile — Sammy Sr. always found baby sitters among the chorus girls who adored his child — but after awhile the bookings thinned out and money was tight. Sammy was three years old when his father wrote to his mother, Rose, asking for a loan. Rose responded by insisting that her son bring Sammy Jr. back home to live with her. It was not a fit life for a young boy to be out on the road practically starving, she felt.

Sammy Sr. had to agree that he was barely able to feed himself, let alone a child. Reluctantly, he came home and handed the boy over to his mother. Rose became the second most important influence in young Sammy's early life, and indeed was more of a parent to him than his biological mother was. As Sammy Sr. hated the idea of being separated for long stretches from the boy he loved, he decided to quit show business and get a "real job" —which would keep him at home with his mother and son.

Sammy did his best to adjust to his new lifestyle out of vaudeville — and the spotlight. He tried driving a taxi for a while, but it was too boring and passive. Washing dishes was even worse. He tried a series of different jobs but none of them could replace the profession he'd loved as much as he loved his son. He reveled in the applause of the audience, in amazing people with his fancy footwork and way with a song. He only felt really alive when he was on stage. He had to go back out on the road. Despite his many different jobs, he'd managed to save up enough money to make this feasible.

Sammy Sr. agonized over how to drop the news to his mother, who was counting on him being a good father to her grandson. He also hated the idea of being separated from Sammy Jr. One afternoon his mother broke out into a dance and little Sammy followed her with a few steps of his own. He seemed to have a natural rhythm and grace that amazed his father. Sammy Sr. was heartened by the display. His boy had obviously inherited his talent, his need to "show off." Show business was also in little

Sammy's blood. His father decided the only thing to do was to add the boy to his act.

Grandma Rose initially wasn't thrilled with this idea. Her son placated her by insisting that they'd stay close to home and always return to her house between bookings. Rose agreed to hide Sammy, who was now five years old and of school age, from truant officers if her son hired a tutor for him while they were out on the road. (Truant officers were assigned to go out and bring in children who were skipping school; their parents could be fined if they kept them at home.)

Things had been tough for Will Mastin since his revue *Holiday in Dixieland* shut down, so Sammy Sr. asked him to form a new act with him and his son. They hired two other dancers and named the group "Four and a Half." Sammy Jr. was the "half." Will Mastin became little Sammy's "Uncle Will;" in subsequent years many people would come to think of him as an actual relation of Sammy Davis Jr., but he wasn't.

Sammy Jr. took to show business right from the start and loved traveling from town to town with his father, Uncle Will,and the rest of the guys and gals. Bookings came easily at first,and all went smoothly — until they reached Michigan. After they finished their act, a grim-faced manager asked them to come to his office. Inside the office was a stern-looking woman who screamed at the two men that they were "exploiting" and "abusing"an innocent youngster. Little Sammy couldn't understand what the fuss was about.

The woman threatened to do her best to close down the theater if the manager didn't fire the Four and a Half act. Sammy loved being part of the show and adored his father and uncle Will, but as far as the woman was concerned he was being "forced" to participate when he should be in school. She was unimpressed when Sammy Sr. mentioned the tutor he'd arranged for his boy. "This is no life for a child that age!" she bellowed.

The manager was too afraid of possible repercussions from employing Four and a Half. He fired the group on the spot. The woman had made a fuss supposedly in the interest of the child, but because of her actions little Sammy — and the four other men in the group — wound up homeless and hungry in freezing cold weather. The woman who started the trouble did nothing to help them.

Their next booking wasn't until a week or two later and they had no place to sleep except the bus terminal. They made soup out of catsup and hot water and tried to make the best of it. A good Samaritan took them home and fed them and eventually they made their way to the next theater on the tour.

In other cities, however, Four and a Half created a small sensation and became a top act — if only on one of the lesser vaudeville circuits. Nevertheless, they were continually employed. Soon other problems cropped up. Sammy Sr. was fond of drink and when he had the money to over-indulge, would become difficult to deal with. He was never pleasant to be around when he was inebriated; little Sammy would recoil from the tension his father created.

Then there was the Geary Society, a group of alleged do-gooders who did their best to see that a law was enforced that forbade anyone under the age of sixteen to appear on the stage. Theater managers tended to think of the Society as a pack of nuisances, and hated their interference. On the other hand, by not complying with the law a theater owner could be fined or have his establishment shut down altogether. Sammy Sr. and Uncle Will — by this time the other two dancers had left the group — tried to get around this by billing young Sammy as the aforementioned "Dancing Midget."

Tales of her son's excessive drinking and the constant threat of the Geary Society got back to Grandma — now called "Mama" Rose by little Sammy — and she made a tough decision. Her grandson's studies were even being neglected and this she would not tolerate. She went after and got custody of Sammy Jr. She had a heart to heart talk with her son and told him that he could take his boy with him on the road only if certain rules and regulations were adhered to. Sammy Sr. had to sharply limit his imbibing of liquor, his son had to have regular tutoring, and his work hours were to be shortened.

Even though Sammy Sr. promised these wishes would be complied with, his mother probably would have kept her grandson at home if he himself had not begged her to let him go. Even at this early age Sammy Jr. was every inch a showman, just like his father.

Two very famous individuals next entered the life of young Sammy Davis Jr. This came about when Sammy Sr. took his son out to Brooklyn where Warner Brothers pictures maintained an east coast studio. Sammy Jr. auditioned for and won a starring role in a "two reeler," or short film, starring the wonderful black entertainer Ethel Waters. In *Rufus Jones for President* (1929) he plays a small boy who decides to run for office. Sammy proved as much a natural actor as he was a dancer. Ethel developed a warm relationship with the boy. Footage of Sammy dancing in this film can be seen in the 1985 film *That's Dancing*, which clearly shows what a wonderful talent he had even at that age. He is adorable,charismatic, and even a bit hammy, but delightfully so. In *That's Entertainment*, he jokes "I can still fit in that suit!"

Sammy's next film role was a small bit in *Season's Greetings* (1930) starring actress Lita Grey and her very famous son, the great comedian Charlie Chaplin. Lita Grey was so charmed by little Sammy that she went to his father and asked if she could adopt him. She could see — even if Sammy Sr. couldn't — that vaudeville was on its way out; all across the country vaudeville theaters were being converted into movie houses. She argued that she could do a lot for the boy and he would have a much bigger chance of amounting to something in Hollywood than on the dying vaudeville circuit. Even if Sammy Sr. could have been talked into giving up his son, which was unlikely, Mama Rose flatly vetoed the idea the minute it was raised. Sammy Jr. belonged with his family, and that was that. Sammy did not appear in any more films until many years later.

Father and son went back on the road with Uncle Willie. Now they were billed as Will Mastin's Gang Featuring Little Sammy. Even in these early days the two older men were beginning to realize that the little boy who so expertly pantomimed their movements and even came up with steps of his own, was the act's draw. The three of them would come out on stage dressed in identical outfits and carrying canes. Even if the hardened audiences were not taken by the now "old hat" routines of Will and Sammy Sr., they were always charmed by cute little Sammy and his sweet, untrained vocalizing. Both men began to realize what a valuable commodity they had in Sammy Jr. Years later this would cause major problems within the group.

In his earliest years, Sammy Davis Jr. had been spared the ugly effects of racism. Most of the white people Sammy had met were perfectly nice to him, show people generally being an open-minded bunch. His father had shielded him whenever he could. There had been times when they were refused service in a restaurant or told that a hotel had no vacancies when that was obviously not the case. Sammy Sr. told his son that they weren't wanted because they were "show people."

Sometimes this was true, particularly when it came to inns and boarding houses. Show people were seen as irresponsible and generally lacking in steady employment. A show could fold and leave the entertainers stranded without money. Sometimes show people would skip out on a hotel bill in the middle of the night. But that didn't explain why waiters would refuse to serve them in certain counties, especially down in the south. One afternoon in the state of Missouri, Sammy Jr. got his answer. As they walked into a restaurant a white waiter sneered at them and told them that "niggers" had to sit in the back.

Sammy then learned that in the eyes of many in the white world he was seen as "different" and "inferior." There were people who would hate him simply because of his skin color, people who had never even met him or knew anything about him. As he got older, he resisted any and all notions that there was anything second-class about him because he was black. The love of his father and grandmother, and his faith in his own abilities, instilled in him a strong sense of self-worth and pride which was never to fail him.

Years went by and Will Mastin's Gang Featuring Little Sammy continued to go from city to city in both the United States and Canada. Vaudeville was hanging on, but it was slowly being edged out not only by films but by the more vulgar burlesque shows. The latter were spicy revues that featured a more ribald type of humor, as well as scantily-clad chorus girls. At least Will Mastin's Gang was by now considered a top act on their circuit; it was continuously making money.

The trouble was that the group was always being booked in third-rate theaters. Prestige — and the top venues — consistently eluded them. This did not matter much to Sammy as he entered his early teens, but the older men could only see that their chances of hitting the Big Time were quickly eroding.

When Sammy was fifteen he had his first encounter with a man who was to have a major impact on his life and career. The group was in Detroit when they received an urgent summons to report to an additional theater where Tommy Dorsey, the famous band leader of the period, was headlining. The act that was supposed to open for Dorsey was detained in another city, and a new act was desperately needed to replace them. Backstage, in between shows, Sammy struck up a conversation with the band's vocalist, a very skinny and friendly fellow named Frank Sinatra, who was destined to become a super-star. Sinatra did not seem to care or notice who was black or who was white — if he liked you, he liked you.

Sinatra had already made some recordings with the Dorsey band, which Sammy had heard. Sammy was much impressed with Sinatra's way of singing, and it influenced his own style for years to come. Sammy did not receive much serious vocal training while on the road, so he studied other singers and picked up what he could until he developed his own style. Neither man had any idea that they'd become very close friends as well as giants of the entertainment industry.

The following year, 1941, the Japanese attacked Pearl Harbor and the United States entered World War Two. Two years later, when he turned eighteen, Sammy was drafted.

The Army would be a whole new world for Sammy Davis Jr., one made up of equal parts courage and despair.

Chapter Two

The Army — and After

While out on the road with his father, Sammy had only had a mild taste of racial discrimination. That all changed when he went into the Army for basic training. He knew what he was in for from the first day when he and the rest of his unit were gathered together in their barracks. There was only one other black soldier in the troop. The corporal immediately segregated the two "nigra's." He moved two cots into a corner and placed them a good way from the rest of the beds, which were normally only two feet apart from one another. Sammy could tell from the corporal's demeanor that neither he nor the other black soldier would be encouraged to fraternize with the other men.

When the sergeant saw what had happened, however, he instructed the corporal to rearrange the beds — Sammy and the other black man would not be segregated from their fellow soldiers. This sergeant was always friendly and helpful to Sammy and made his life in the Army much easier that it might have been. There were also many other white soldiers who were not prejudiced. They saw Sammy as just another "dogface" who might soon be shipped out to fight for his country along with them.

Sammy was a very personable man and he liked to be friendly with everybody. On some occasions this was his undoing. A private named Jennings called him over to a group of his pals one day and asked Sammy if he wanted a beer. Sammy thought, "at last, the thaw is melting," and sat down in a proffered chair. Everyone was smiling at him and he thought these men were at last in a frame of mind to accept him. They handed him a big mug of beer. Smiling, Sammy took a swallow and immediately spit out the putrid liquid. It was urine.

Sammy was astounded by the ugliness of the men's actions, and enraged as well. Although much smaller than the other soldiers, Sammy's dancing and athletic ability made him a worthy opponent. He blackened more than one eye after tasting the "beer." When the sergeant found out what had provoked Sammy's violent behavior, he spared him any punishment; it was the gang of nasty jokesters who went to the guardhouse. Jennings and his buddies swore that they'd get even with him. The sergeant warned Sammy to watch his back.

Prejudice is generally caused by an inferiority complex. A well-adjusted person who has pride in himself and faith in his abilities, who recognizes his or her self-worth, will not need to feel superior to entire groups of people. Since a person who is racist, anti-Semitic or homophobic senses deep down that he is not really superior to whichever group he has chosen, he begins to fear and despise all members of said group. In extreme cases this hatred can lead to violence. Jennings was a prime example of this kind of insecure bigot.

Some nights later Sammy received a message that his sympathetic sergeant wanted to meet with him at an isolated barracks at the edge of the camp. The message was a phony. Unsuspecting, he went to keep the rendezvous, only to find himself surrounded by Jennings and his friends. Before he could get away, too far from anyone to call for help, he was thrown to the ground and held down. Using a paint brush, Jennings first wrote the word "coon" on Sammy's forehead. Then he and the others took up buckets of white paint and splashed them all over the helpless man's face and clothing. "This is what people should look like, nigger!" they shouted at him.

This was the worst experience of anti-black hatred that Sammy had ever endured. The sergeant and many of the other white privates were completely sympathetic to him and outraged at what Jennings and the others had done. The sergeant took Sammy under his wing, encouraged him to study and borrow books from his personal library, and did a lot to convince him that not all white people were bad or narrow-minded. However, it deeply disturbed Sammy that men like Jennings were supposed to be his fellow soldiers fighting against a common enemy overseas. As far as Sammy was concerned, *they* were the enemy. How could he convince people like Jennings that he wasn't so bad? Failing that, how could he at least triumph over their prejudiced attitudes?

The sergeant gave him a possible answer when he found out that Sammy had been a song and dance man in his life outside the service. "Why don't you appear in some variety shows at the Service Club?" he asked Sammy. The Service Club put on shows on a regular basis to keep the men from becoming bored. They had not yet been called into combat — the fighting overseas was winding down — although there was always that possibility. Sammy himself had a mild heart arrhythmia which probably would have been enough to keep him stateside.

Sammy loved the idea of entertaining, but he was not certain he could face such a potentially hostile audience. He was afraid there were more men like Jennings in the camp than like the Sergeant. Not every biased soldier went out of his way to attack Sammy like Jennings and his friends did, but they might not make it pleasant for him if he came out to do a number for them in the show. He revealed his fears to the sergeant, who leveled with him that it would be better for him to take his chances than to completely back out of doing something that would bring him – and possibly many enlisted men — great enjoyment. Sammy agreed to appear in the show.

To his amazement, he was an instant sensation. The privates couldn't help but admire his great tap-dancing skills, his smooth way with a song, the sheer joy and exuberance he exhibited while performing. Sammy was wise enough to know that just because they admired his showmanship did not mean all the men would go on ignoring his skin color once the show was over. He knew that to many of them he was little more than a court jester, a prancing Negro fool, albeit a talented one. But while he was on that stage he was somebody; he could not be disdained or overlooked even if he had wanted to be.

Sammy realized then that his talent was the only thing he could really count on in the world. It would be his weapon against prejudice. It would be his ticket out of the swamp of second-class citizenship and into the stratosphere of respect and power. Sammy knew what a dire trap poverty could be, especially for the black man, how it wore you down and limited your options. Someday he swore his talent would make him wealthier and more admired than all of his detractors put together.

But he had to face facts. Once the war was over and he got out of the service, he would still be just one member of a trio of vaudevillians on a third-rate touring circuit. If his dreams were to come true, if he were ever to triumph over these little men and their petty, ugly prejudices, he would have to do better than that.

After he received his honorable discharge, Sammy prepared to go on tour again with what was now called the Will Mastin Trio. Will and his father had lined up plenty of bookings, so neither work nor money would be scarce. Still, Sammy knew how far down the ladder he was when he turned on the radio in their hotel room in Los

Angeles. Tuning in the popular show *Your Hit Parade*, the first voice he heard was a familiar one: Frank Sinatra.

By now Sinatra had left Dorsey's band and found even greater success as a solo. He had thousands of girls screaming their hearts and lungs out at his every note and appearance. In other words, in the intervening years since Sammy and Frank had first met, Sinatra had become a star.

Sammy wanted the life and career of a Sinatra, but it seemed impossible. There were, of course, many black stars even during this period — Ethel Waters, The Nicholas Brothers, Lena Horne, the Mills Brothers — but they appeared on the bill in major venues, not in small-time markets as did the Will Mastin Trio. Wanting to bask in some reflected glory, Sammy went down to the studio from where *Your Hit Parade* was broadcast. Outside the studio amidst a throng of young people, he waited for Sinatra's autograph just like all the others.

Sinatra thought Sammy looked familiar the moment he set eyes on him. They compared memories about the gig in Detroit, and renewed their friendship. Sinatra gave Sammy free passes to the show, and invited him backstage to his dressing room where he held court amongst his many admirers. Sammy was struck by the fact that although Frank wasn't that much older than most of his fans, he seemed more mature, more dynamic, "like a King," as he remembered.

It was shortly afterward that Sammy got news from his father that the Will Mastin Trio had for once been booked into a major new venue, the El Rancho Hotel and Casino in Las Vegas, Nevada. Las Vegas was only just beginning to turn into the gambling capital of the USA during this period, but there was a great need for entertainers of all types. It was exciting time to be in Nevada, and the Will Mastin Trio arrived in town with high hopes.

Sammy fully expected that they would be given rooms in the hotel, but were told in no uncertain terms that "Negroes" — even the hotel's entertainers — were not permitted to stay in the rooms or even enter the casino. This was similar to the outrageous policy of the famous nightspot the Cotton Club in New York's Harlem. Blacks were allowed to entertain there, but they could not sit in the audience as customers. Las Vegas may have been a hot, "happening" spot for people in show business, but it was the Same Old Story as far as Blacks were concerned.

Of course, white entertainers at the El Rancho would receive free room and board for as long as they worked in the hotel. Sammy was reminded once again of his second-class status and he hated it. The management of El Rancho directed Sammy and the others to a "colored" section of town where they could find rooms to rent.

Here the situation was even worse. Not only was the dilapidated house they found three rooms in a far cry from the luxury of El Rancho, the black woman who rented the place wanted nearly twice as much money as the El Rancho would have charged. It was bad enough that their income from the gig would decrease because they had to pay rent each week, but such a high rent would really reduce their profits.

"How can you do this to your own people?" Sammy's father asked the landlady. "I gotta make a livin' myself," was her reply. As disgusted as they were, the Trio had no choice but to take the rooms. There was nothing cheaper to be had and the other big hotels would not accept "colored folk," either. Although the money they had counted on making in Las Vegas would now be diminished, they still hoped appearing at the El Rancho would have a positive effect on their careers.

It did. They attracted the attention of a scout connected to the prestigious RKO circuit, which could get them bookings into much better places than they were used to — and at much higher fees. They were also hired as the opening act on a post-war stage show put together by actor Mickey Rooney. Rooney and Davis were both short guys who were giants when you factored in talent, and they became fast friends. Like Frank Sinatra, Rooney had no patience with racist attitudes and punched out some drunken guys who came to a party and hurled racial epithets at Sammy and his partners. Mickey tried to get Sammy a small role in a film he was doing but another actor was hired.

And then there was Sinatra, who had never forgotten Sammy and made up his mind to help him. Sinatra was a highly talented man, a musical genius, who was not jealous of other talent, but rather worshipped it. Although he had assorted personality flaws, including a short temper, Sinatra was a friend for life once he was in your corner. If Sammy had not had talent, Sinatra probably would not — and could not — have done that much for him. Friends of Sammy's opened doors, but he marched through on his own two dancing feet. Sinatra was instrumental in getting The Will Mastin Trio the biggest break of their careers.

Sammy could not believe the news when his father told him: they had been hired to be the opening act for Frankie at the Capitol Theater in New York. They would be

Sammy Davis Jr. in the early days of his brilliant carrer.

making over a thousand dollars a week, a heady sum for the 1940's. Sammy figured that Frank had to have something to do with it (although their recent emergence from the third-rate vaudeville circuit couldn't have hurt), but it wasn't much later that he learned from a booking agent that Sinatra had insisted on using the trio — or else. He had also made sure they got the kind of money that other opening acts — white opening acts — always got. Sinatra's advisers wanted to go with a much better-known group, but Sinatra was boss.

Appearing in New York in one of the biggest theaters of a major entertainment chain was the top of the line for any act like the Will Mastin Trio. It seemed as if Sammy Sr.'s insistence on dragging Little Sammy into show business had paid off. Although he and Uncle Will might have been loathe to admit it, deep down they and everyone knew that it was Sammy's energy and dynamism that had taken them to the top. Sammy Sr. and Will both knew it might have been a very different story if young Sammy had not been part of the act. And there was always the lurking fear of what might happen to the two older men if Sammy decided to break out on his own.

But for this major break at the Capitol they would have to thank Sinatra, which is why Sammy virtually worshipped the man for the rest of his life. Sinatra had a strong commitment to civil rights and did not see blacks as inferior. Given the times, his stance could have had a negative effect on his career, but this made no difference to Sinatra. One time Sammy tried to get into the famous

Copacabana nightclub to see Frank, but the doorman had him ejected because he was black. When Sinatra found out, he sent Sammy a personal invitation, told the club management that his friend had better get in, and made sure there were plenty of other friends to sit with Sammy at the prominent front table.

In addition, Sinatra was not intimidated by other people with talent, such as Sammy, and indeed helped them when he could. For these and many other reasons Sammy remained loyal to Sinatra and praised him to the skies. They did have more than one falling out, however, but were always eventually reconciled.

This was only the beginning. Now that they had Sinatra in their corner, and had played in top-of-the-line venues, Sammy and company would be seen by the "right" people — that is, people who were in a position to get them bigger and better bookings. There would be no stopping The Will Mastin Trio. Sammy Davis Jr. would have an even greater success than he had ever imagined.

But first would come a devastating incident that would nearly end his career — and his life — in one shattering instant.

Chapter Three

Smash Up

Now that the Will Mastin Trio had played the Capital, there was no place that wasn't open to them. They even played the Copacabana, the very place that Sammy had been refused admittance to because of his color. (Sinatra had forced the management to change their policy permanently.) After hitting all the top nightspots on the east coast, the trio went west to California. In Los Angeles, they played such tony venues as Ciro's and Slapsy Maxie's.

Their engagement at Slapsy Maxie's served to introduce them to the major players of Hollywood. Sinatra, who had already appeared in a number of movies by this time, invited every star he knew personally and quite a few he didn't to the opening night. Among the stars in attendance was Humphrey Bogart and his wife, Lauren

Bacall, who held boozy gatherings in their home in the Holmby Hills on a regular basis.

Meeting Sammy backstage, "Bogie" and "Bacall", as they were known, asked him to drop by any time he cared to. After that he became a semi-regular at what was called the parties of the "Holmby Hills Rat Pack." The group was so christened after Bacall referred to a group of bedraggled regulars as a "pack of rats" when they came back from a late-night jaunt elsewhere,

The elite of Hollywood talent gathered at Bogie and Bacall's. Starstruck Sammy saw not only his pal Sinatra, but everyone from singer-actress Judy Garland of *The Wizard of Oz* fame to the dapper playwright and entertainer Noel Coward from England. Every once in a while the talented guests would break out into an impromptu song or dance number, and Sammy would follow up by wowing them with his fancy footwork. During this time Sammy saw himself as "a fringe member of the rat pack."

It was Humphrey Bogart who put his finger on the basic problem with the Will Mastin Trio. Bogie had had a few drinks before he went backstage to congratulate the fellows during a later engagement at Ciro's, another popular Los Angeles nightspot. Tactlessly, he told

Sammy's father and Uncle Will that they should retire and leave the singing and dancing to Sammy! "The kid's the whole show," he told them.

Noting the stricken, embarrassed looks on the older men's faces, Bogart apologized, but in truth he had only stated the belief of most in the audience. Sammy Sr. and Will were not untalented, but they relied too much on stale old routines and did not have Sammy Jr.'s sheer genius and unparalleled energy. It looked more and more like Sammy was simply carrying the two older men who contributed less and less to the act.

A tape of the three men appearing on the Colgate Summer Comedy Hour in the fifties tells the story. It isn't that Will or Sammy Sr. were complete zeros — both could dance quite well if not as good as Sammy — but they lacked Sammy's outgoing personality and charisma. Sammy is so appealing and likable, and even looks so handsome, on television, that the two older men almost inevitably fade into the background. A firecracker of dynamism and talent — Sammy does wonderful impressions and even plays the drums expertly — it was clear he just didn't need them.

Knowing that it was Sammy who brought in the crowds, they were content to hand him props, sing backup, and tap dance a little as he performed most of the numbers. Everything about him screamed "Big Time!" while Will and his father were still a second-rate vaudeville team pretending they were something much greater.

By this time Sammy had started doing song numbers, and he was a much better vocalist than his father or Will. The two older men could carry a tune, but they had no real singing style like Sammy did. Sammy had also begun adding impressions to the act since their appearances in Las Vegas. He could do uncanny imitations of virtually anyone in show business. At first he imitated other singers, such as Nat King Cole, Tony Bennett, and Vaughn Monroe, then graduated to such actors as Jimmy Cagney, James Stewart, and Cary Grant.

A brilliant impressionist, he was able to completely erase his natural "black sound" when required and do dead-on imitations of virtually anyone he encountered, black or white. Some impressionists can only target the broader characteristics of the people they imitate, but Sammy could get down to the subtleties. In his nightclub act years later he would wow the audience by having "Humphrey Bogart," "Cary Grant," "Marlon Brandon" (as the Godfather!), "Dean Martin," and even "Jerry Lewis"

Sammy looks pensive in this portrait taken during the height of his solo career.

all sing "Rockabye Your Baby" in rapid succession.

There was something else about Sammy that set him

apart from other entertainers, especially black ones. Many black artists in this period, especially when they performed for a primarily white audience, would downplay their intelligence. Also, they would never interact in any way with the very people they were entertaining. It was almost as if they were just grateful to be allowed to sing and dance and wanted to get off the stage without calling attention to themselves and certainly not to their race.

Sammy noticed that, however good a black entertainer's grammar might be backstage, once he was on stage he would speak stereotypical "jive" or "eubonics." Furthermore, he might dopily shuffle around and pop out his eyes because he figured that was what white audiences expected of a "colored person." Sammy's father and Will adhered to this policy and explained that it was better not to rock the boat or appear too smart or "uppity." Sammy, on the other hand, thought it was a mistake not to connect with an audience, of any color.

Once it was established that he was the leader of the act (although neither his father nor Will would quite acknowledge this), Sammy spoke right to the members of the audience. He did not downplay the fact that he was black, but often made references to it in a joking — but never angry or jarring – fashion. He told little stories about himself and his partners the way other entertainers did. He wanted the audience to see him not just as a "colored person" but as a full human being who was not all that different from the rest of them. Not only did he feel this was an important step in the direction of racial equality, but he saw it as being essential to a successful show business career.

Sammy was later accused of overdoing the "grammatical correctness." Catching his act and then becoming chums with him, comedian Jerry Lewis warned Sammy that if he spoke better than everyone in the audience, white or black, he would come off as condescending. Sammy's intention had been to show that a black man could speak as well as anyone, but Lewis felt he had gone too much to the other extreme. How could the often down-to-earth members of a night club audience relate to someone who spoke all the time as if he thought he were quoting Shakespeare?

Lewis also advised Sammy that his father and Will were coming off like his stooges. It was a combination of Sammy's "grand" manner toward them and the fact that the two older men had less to do and were easily outshone by Sammy. Sammy took Jerry's advice, and made them a more integral part of the act. He never entirely shed that certain "grand" way of speaking, however.

Yet it was his patter to the audience between numbers that made him seem like a fresh and exciting new personality compared to his two partners. Sammy knew that talent and looks was only ten percent of it; the other ninety per cent was chemistry. It was crucial to have the audience relate to, and therefore, *like* you. He had seen talented acts fall by the wayside because the performer's personality was simply too distant or off-putting. As for looks, Sammy was never satisfied with his appearance, and never quite accepted that he was handsome in his own unique way.

He decided he'd keep too busy on the stage for people to contemplate his looks. If the audience liked you, he figured, you could be downright ugly and they wouldn't care.

The Will Mastin Trio, now Starring Sammy Davis Jr., continued to play the finest clubs and theaters across the country. They were also making records which were climbing the charts; Sammy also did solo recordings. In 1946 his recording of *The Way You Look Tonight* was named Record of the Year and Sammy named Most Outstanding New Personality. Every top venue in New

York, Las Vegas, Los Angeles and elsewhere bid for the services of the trio.

They were now well enough known that they did not need to open for Sinatra; people were opening for them. On more than one occasion when they had been hired to open for somebody else, they received so much more applause and curtain calls than the featured act that the management made them the stars instead. Naturally this did not make them popular with the former headliners. Speaking of which, as Sammy got bigger, Sinatra got smaller. Most of his fans, teenaged girls, had moved on to other idols, and Sinatra was no longer packing them in like he'd done before.

During a gig in Manhattan, Sammy was chilled and saddened to see Frank walking down Broadway completely unrecognized, ignored. No one even wanted his autograph. Sammy wanted to console the man but was afraid he'd be too embarrassed to be seen this way by a peer. Eventually Sinatra got back on top by being nominated for an Oscar for his performance in *From Here to Eternity* in 1953. Sinatra would continue to play an important part in Sammy's life in the years to come.

In 1954 the Will Mastin Trio was playing the New Frontier Hotel and Casino in Las Vegas. This time they were given first-class treatment, including rooms in the hotel and free chips to play with in the casino. They were paid $7500 a week. Sammy had his pick of women. He was truly on the top of the world and loving every minute of it. One night he asked his dresser, Charlie, to drive him to Los Angeles for an early morning appointment. Sammy was going to record some vocals for a movie soundtrack. Sammy loved the idea of having an appointment in Hollywood.

As they started out in Sammy's beautiful new Cadillac, he thought about what it would be like to drive through the gates of a major movie studio. He had certainly come far, hadn't he? When the trip was half over, Sammy told Charlie that he would spell him. He turned on the radio and smiled with pleasure as he heard his own voice singing *Hey, There!* Yes, "Little Sammy" sure was going places, wasn't he?

A car ahead of him was moving erratically and Sammy realized with shock that the woman who was driving was going to attempt a U-turn on a high speed parkway! Other cars were moving this way and that to make room for her as she actually swung the car around, pulling frantically at the wheel. Sammy did his best to maneuver so that he wouldn't hit either the woman or any of the cars on either side of him. He put his foot down hard on the brake but saw with dismay that there was no way he could keep from hitting the woman's car. He braced himself for the impact. There came a sudden terrific jolt — and then total blackness.

When Sammy regained consciousness, Charlie was bleeding horribly and pointing at his employer's face. Sammy felt something wet and mushy on his cheekbone and realized it was one of his eyes! Sammy held on to the eye and tried to pretend that none of this was happening to him. He heard sirens in the distance. He was too much in shock to feel pain, only a terrible blankness. He worried if Charlie would be okay, if everything would be okay from then on. Ambulances arrived and rushed the two men to the hospital. No one in the car that had caused the accident was hurt.

Sammy woke up the next day to learn that his eye had been removed. Although he had undergone surgery, there was no way the doctors could have saved it. There was now an artificial eye made of plastic in the socket. His father and Will came to visit him, but it was like being at a wake. A funeral for the Will Mastin Trio. Sammy was alive but he was convinced his career in show business was dead. When his visitors were gone he tried not to think that his meteoric rise had been cruelly and unexpectedly cut off through no fault of his own.

Frank Sinatra came to the hospital to give Sammy a pep talk. Other friends and relatives told him he must not think negatively. The eye patch he wore looked dashing, he was told, and he fiddled with the idea of leaving the patch on for good. But the main problem was that now that he had only one eye, it might affect his equilibrium. He could learn to adjust to seeing the world through one eye instead of two, but could he do the kind of twisting, complex, energetic dance steps he'd done before without falling on his face?

The Will Mastin Trio honored their bookings, but without Sammy. Actor Jeff Chandler and others took over for him while he recuperated. It killed Sammy to be inactive, out of the spotlight, letting time pass until everyone who'd once known him might forget him. He made up his mind that he could not let this lousy break stop him from continuing toward his goals. The pep talks from Sinatra and others had done much good, but as usual it was Sammy himself who got back in the game.

With a lot of practice and determination, it wasn't too long before he was ready to resume work. Having one eye would not be the problem he had been afraid it would be.

Once he got used to his unique way of looking at the world, he could dance just as well as before. But for quite a while Sammy was sure that he would lose everything he had achieved up until that point.

Popular Jewish comedian Eddie Cantor put Sammy on his TV show, which reached millions more people than his appearances in clubs and casinos. When the Cantor show got hate mail from racists, Cantor put Sammy on again. Cantor's sponsors tried to dissuade him from having Davis as a guest star in the future; Cantor responded by practically making Sammy a semi-regular. A victim of prejudice himself, Cantor was not about to knuckle under to bigoted reactions.

Sammy eventually converted to Judaism, partly because the many Jews he met understood the plight of blacks better than the average white man. But he also studied Jewish teachings and philosophy and came to agree with much of it. He was accused of converting simply because so many powerful people in show business, people who could help him, were Jewish. In other words, it was seen as a cynical career move. Others felt that Sammy had to be different or die. But Sammy's conversion was genuine, and not entered into lightly. In 1965, the Jewish Association B'nai B'rith named him their

Sammy was one of the first entertainers to headline in Las Vegas; here he poses with a bevy of show girls.

Man of the Year. He was also awarded the Cultural Achievement Award of the State of Israel in the 1970's.

Sammy was his own boss. He did what he wanted and

didn't care what people thought. Friends of his chided him that now that he was a Jew he'd be discriminated against on two counts. He answered that people now had twice as many reasons to hate him. He was not about to let prejudice of any sort keep him from getting what he wanted out of life.

Sammy had now appeared in the best of theaters, night clubs and casinos. He'd been on radio and television, and made recordings. He'd even been in the movies when he was much younger.

There was only one thing in the entertainment industry left for Sammy Davis Jr. to conquer.

But that was going to be quite a challenge.

Chapter Four

Mr. Wonderful

Sammy was delighted to learn that top New York producers were interested in starring him in a new Broadway show, *Mr. Wonderful,* in 1956. The only catch was that his father and "Uncle Will" would appear in the show along with him. Although Sammy was itching to be a solo act instead of the heart and soul of a trio, at this point in time he would not have considered leaving the other two men behind. He knew as well as anyone that the Will Mastin Trio was nothing without him.

Even the show's producers told Sammy that it was time he struck out on his own, but Sammy did not want to seem disloyal. Therefore *Mr. Wonderful* actually starred "the Will Mastin Trio featuring Sammy Davis Jr." Other cast members included veteran comedian Jack Carter, singer-dancer Chita Rivera, and Olga James, who had appeared with Dorothy Dandridge in the film *Carmen Jones* two years previously.

Initially Sammy loved the show's concept. He would play a black entertainer very much like himself who decides he would have better odds at success in a country where there was less prejudice — for instance, France. He moves to Paris, plays the most prestigious nightclubs, and revels in the fact that in Europe his color seems of little importance. But he has a crisis of conscience when he encounters an old friend who tells him that by leaving the United States he has only run away from his problems, not solved them. His friend urges him to return to the country of his birth and try to make it there despite the increased odds against it.

Sammy loved the conflict that the story set up for his character, Charley, to face. Was success worth being virtually exiled from your friends, family, and nation? How could he give up the good, new life he had in Paris for one of doubt and struggle back home? Would things ever be better for blacks in general if each man refused to take a stand and fight for change? These were crises that Sammy himself had struggled with, and he looked forward to such weighty matters — important issues to all

Americans and especially blacks — being examined on the usually frivolous Broadway stage.

Matters of prejudice, race, and other important issues had been dealt with in previous Broadway shows, such as Kern and Hammerstein's *Show Boat* (from which comes the anthem "Old Man River") and Rodgers and Hammerstein's *South Pacific*. However, Sammy rightly saw that as originally conceived *Mr. Wonderful* would, unlike those previous shows, deal with the current, modern-day plight of the Black Man in America. Unfortunately, he was to discover that the time just wasn't right.

The show was performed out of town and right away the producers saw the problem. Some critics and audiences, of course, were simply uncomfortable with any message of racial equality. They wanted blacks to sing and dance for them, not consider themselves equals. But even the more liberal members of the audience and critical establishment noted that *Mr. Wonderful* delivered its message with the subtlety of a sledge hammer. They argued that audiences went to Broadway shows to be entertained, not to hear a lecture.

Show Boat made its points about racial inequality without coming right out and saying anything about it.

South Pacific sang its message in just one number —
You've Got to Be Carefully Taught — and then let it
alone. The original script for *Mr. Wonderful* made the
same points over and over and over again.

Too afraid of losing their audience entirely — not to
mention their investment — the producers of *Mr.
Wonderful* made serious changes to the story and cut out
virtually anything that smacked of moralizing. By the time
it opened on Broadway the show was simply the story of
an aspiring entertainer (who just happens to be black) who
can't decide whether or not he wants to leave his small
town and its limited options for New York. "Some
conflict!" Sammy snickered. "Why wouldn't the guy want
to go to New York? Where else would somebody go who
wants to make it in the "theater?" The character's race was
rarely if ever alluded to.

The producers of the show had made it clear to Sammy
that he could not simply recreate his club act on Broadway
and expect to attract a huge audience. They gave his
father and Will small roles in the show, and even a number
to do with Sammy (a wild jazz number called "Jacques
d'Iraque"), but otherwise the two older men were shunted
to the side.

Sammy Sr. and Mastin saw the handwriting on the

wall. They agreed not to raise a fuss about the situation if Sammy signed a contract agreeing to split all of his future income three ways; this was regardless of whether or not the two other men were hired for the same gig. Even after the two older men retired, Sammy was splitting his salary with them. He was grateful to his father and Will for the opportunities they'd given him, for all he'd learned from them, but as the years went by he came to resent working so hard to support them as they lounged around doing nothing.

Mr. Wonderful opened to mostly good reviews. By this time Sammy had developed into a very talented vocalist as well as dancer, and his numbers were a highlight of the show. These included a nice duet with Olga James entitled *"Ethel Baby,"* a big, snappy production number called *Too Close for Comfort* during which Sammy indulged in some tap-dancing, and his nicely-sung solo ballad, *There.*

Sammy brought down the house with another production number, *Sing you Sinners.* This last number was the only one from the show to become a standard (although Sammy often performed *Too Close for Comfort* in later years), although perhaps the best number is the title tune, sung by Olga James. Most of the songs were composed by Jerry Bock, who would later have a major success with the musical *Fiddler on the Roof*. While not as famous nor popular as that super-smash, *Mr. Wonderful* nevertheless became a hit show, in large part due to Sammy's truly "wonderful" performance.

There are those who say that Sammy developed a star "attitude" while appearing in *Mr. Wonderful;* later he would come to agree with them. After the show was over, he was so hepped up and energized that he couldn't go to sleep even if he wanted to. He had been a night owl for most of his life — working in night clubs meant that you slept in most of the day — but now he insisted his associates from the show keep him company until dawn. Chita Rivera and others were virtually ordered to come to his apartment to play games and have drinks until Sammy felt like going to bed. He would not take no for an answer. His stardom had gone to his head. He was going to be the "Life of the Party" and you were going to be part of his entourage whether you liked it or not.

Sammy would also insist that a gang from the show and other friends accompany him on jaunts to bars and clubs in the wee hours of the evening. He wanted to be recognized, he needed his stardom to be acknowledged. He was no longer the battered, soaked-with-white-paint little black boy who'd been continually mistreated in the Army. He was not the soldier who had to sing and dance to win approval. He was a bona fide *star* and he wanted everyone to know it.

Many high-hat Manhattan night clubs that would not open their doors to blacks — and to working-class whites — received the big Broadway star with open arms. He broke the color barrier at night spot after night spot. There was only one dragon he was never quite able to defeat, and that was the snooty east side supper club El Morocco.

Sammy was holding court at his apartment one night when one of his guests suggested it might be nice to go out instead of playing the usual games. Someone picked up the phone and tried to make a reservation at El Morocco for "Sammy Davis Jr. and party." Then they patiently explained that Sammy was the star of *Mr. Wonderful*. Ironically, music from the show was being played by the club's orchestra even as this conversation took place. The management of the club made it clear without coming right out and saying so that it would be better for Mr. Davis and party to go elsewhere.

There was more than just the club's racist policies for Sammy to contend with. Many clubs and casinos were opening their doors to black customers for the first time in history because Sammy insisted upon it, or he'd refuse to perform. Sammy was a big drawer now, and the night clubs knew it — so they complied. It was also true that Sammy had worked hard to make it to the top and wanted all of the privileges he felt should be accorded a star, including a prominent table at El Morocco.

Sure, he and his friends could go to the more bohemian establishments in Greenwich Village where nobody cared about your color, religion, or even sexual orientation. But a star should be able to go anywhere, he insisted. He had been accepted, sometimes warmly ushered into, some of the best night spots in Manhattan, so he was not about to let El Morocco off the hook.

Sammy chose an odd time to step up the battle against the supper club. He was attending the closing night party of *Mr. Wonderful*, when he suddenly asked two white friends of his who frequented the place to get in a cab with him and ride uptown. Part of him had been hoping that the earlier brush-off by phone had been a simple misunderstanding. Perhaps he should have spoken to the maitre d' himself. Perhaps the club thought that the friend who called was a little drunk and playing a joke. Surely they'd have a different attitude when Sammy Davis Jr. himself walked into the foyer?

This was not the case. He and his friends were shown to a table, but it was way in back in a section reserved for out of towners and "nobodies." No one greeted him or fawned over him. He felt devalued not only as a black man but as a person. It was as much his ego that was affronted as his pride in being black. After a few minutes of agonized embarrassment, he stormed out of the club in a rage. The incident only reminded him that no matter how high you got in life, there was always someone out there who would not accept you. He deeply regretted not fighting harder to make *Mr. Wonderful* the strong story of racial pride that it had once been intended to be.

When *Mr. Wonderful* ended its run, Sammy found little time to stew over the slight at El Morocco. By the late fifties, his father and Will Mastin finally decided to put the "Trio" to rest and let Sammy continue as a solo. They certainly had no reason to complain, as Sammy would remain the breadwinner in the family. Sammy continued his club engagements, entertained at casinos, and appeared in a film or two. These included *Anna Lucasta* (1958), the second film version of a play by Philip Yordan, and *Porgy and Bess* (1959). He also found time to get married.

Sammy's first marriage was a sad, shabby affair that in

later years Sammy did not like to be reminded of. One night while bar-hopping with friends, he impulsively proposed to a pretty black show girl named Loray White who was several years his junior. Loray was a perfectly sweet woman who, unfortunately, took the drunken proposal very seriously. Sammy went ahead with the wedding, hoping for the best, but his career and his pursuit of the high life would always take precedence. The "marriage" lasted only a few months. He paid Loray a generous settlement, and the two never saw each other again. It might have lasted longer if Sammy had been in love, but that was not the case.

In 1958 Sammy appeared on TV's *GE Theater* in a teleplay entitled *Auf Weidersen*. In his first dramatic role he is a bit self-conscious but not bad as an Army private interacting with orphans in Germany. His two 1950's film roles varied in quality. *Anna Lucasta* was perceived as a vehicle for Eartha Kitt, who played the title role, a prostitute. Her mannered performance destroyed Kitt's chances of becoming a film star, and Sammy's reviews were mixed. Rex Ingram got the best notices as Anna's father. However, in the supporting role of Sportin' Life in *Porgy and Bess*, Sammy nearly walked off with the picture.

Porgy and Bess was a film adaptation of George Gershwin's American folk opera. The film re-teamed the star (Dorothy Dandridge) and director (Otto Preminger) of *Carmen Jones*, which was also based on a famous opera. Dandridge and Preminger had been romantically involved while filming *Carmen Jones*, but things had turned sour by the time of *Porgy and Bess*. This made for tense, unpleasant moments on the set when the bad-tempered Preminger took out his anger on Dorothy. Dandridge was to have co-starred with Harry Belafonte, her romantic lead in *Carmen Jones*, but Belafonte objected to the storyline and was replaced by Sidney Poitier. Sammy recalled that Dorothy understandably seemed remote all through the filming, although he had lots of laughs with Pearl Bailey and others in the cast.

Porgy and Bess was the story of poor, downtrodden, uneducated blacks living in a ramshackle community in the 1920's. Many blacks in the 1950's, such as Belafonte, objected to the portrayal and saw it as a step backwards. Others recognized that *Porgy and Bess*, whatever its flaws, was an authentic American musical masterpiece and would never be taken as the "last word" on blacks in this country. Catfish Row, where the story took place, was only one community during one point in history.

"I Can Do Anything"

Sammy may have respected the objections made by others to the movie, but he never seriously considered not appearing in it. It was a major career break for him. Although Sportin' Life was only a supporting part, Sammy received star billing along with Dandridge and Poitier, probably due to his sensational Broadway stint and the

Sammy as Sportin' Liffe from *Porgy and Bess*, here recreated for a TV special some years after the film was made.

publicity it engendered. It didn't hurt that friend Frank Sinatra, who was now back on top as a film star and recording artist, put in a good word with studio chief Samuel Goldwyn.

The character of Sportin' Life is a sharp-talking cocaine ("happy dust") dealer with an eye for the ladies and a good time. In some ways he can be seen as the serpent slithering through a God-fearing community and egging people on to do evil. Like most serpents, he has a lot of surface charm and appeal, which was easy for the likable Sammy to approximate. Sportin' Life appears throughout the opera and the movie to stir up trouble now and then, and plays a major role at the finale.

Bess has fled from her abusive lover Crown into the arms of the more sympathetic Porgy, who later kills Crown in self-defense. Porgy is taken to jail and Sportin' Life sees the opportunity to move in on Bess. He convinces her that Porgy will never get out of prison and she should come with him to New York. When the freed Porgy arrives back in Catfish Row and discovers what has happened, he makes up his mind to pursue Bess to the big city and win her back. The opera ends as he sings of his intentions and leaves his home for a hopeful if uncertain future.

Sammy gave a sensational performance as Sportin' Life, and impressed audiences and critics with his dancing and his vocalizing of the famous tune *It Ain't Necessarily So,* among others. There was talk that he might be nominated for an Oscar, but he was undone by his billing. He could not be nominated for a supporting Oscar, because he was one of the film's stars. And he couldn't be nominated for a starring Oscar, because his role was too small. Sammy was greatly disappointed by this turn of events, but gratified at how well received both he and the picture were by the public and critics.

As for Sinatra, in the years ahead Sammy's and Frank's lives would come crashing together time and again in unexpected ways.

Chapter Five

Running With the Pack

Although he was disappointed not to receive an Oscar nod for *Porgy and Bess*, Sammy was bolstered by some good news from old pal, Frank Sinatra. Sinatra wanted him to appear in a film with him entitled *Never So Few* (1959) for the tidy sum of $75,000. The film explored the bloody conflict between American troops and Japanese in the Kachin Hills of North Burma.

Sinatra had had to fight MGM studios over the casting of Davis. The part, an Army jeep driver, was tiny and did not seem to justify such a big star and large expense. But Sinatra had such clout with the studio that he got both Sammy and another friend, actor Peter Lawford, juicy fees for small roles. At least that was the way it was supposed to work out. Then came the infamous radio interview that almost ended the friendship between Sammy and Sinatra for good.

Sammy certainly had many reasons to be grateful to Sinatra. Although Sinatra could be a good friend to people he liked and admired, he also had a formidable ego. For years it had always stuck in Sammy's craw that Sinatra unconsciously patronized him; he gave off the vibe that his was the superior talent. Sammy was wise enough to know that Sinatra would hardly have boosted him if he hadn't recognized his, Sammy's, abilities, but Frank always acted as if Sammy were the "little guy" who would have gotten nowhere without Frank's help. Sammy was grateful for the part in. *Never so Few* even as he was insulted that it was such a nothing role, practically a walk-on.

As far as Sammy was concerned, Frank did not acknowledge the years of hard work — and his way with an audience — that had garnered Sammy so many fans. Sammy was also bothered by the cruel taunts and vicious behavior indulged in by Frank when the man had too much to drink. Occasionally Sinatra would make cutting remarks to Sammy — and many others — that the next morning he would forget he had said .

Sammy was remarkably indiscreet about these matters when he appeared on Jack Eigen's radio show in Chicago shortly before filming on *Never So Few* was to begin. Goaded on by Eigen, Sammy admitted that sometimes

Sinatra could "treat people rotten" and that his "talent was no excuse." He insisted that he himself was the "number one" singer in the country, not Sinatra. Sammy was indeed very popular at this point, but he was not quite as famous or beloved as the "Chairman of the Board," as Frank was known. On the other hand, he was often billed as "America's Greatest Entertainer," and he was intensely proud of the appellation.

If Sammy had made these statements to a mutual friend and Frank had found out about it he might have been somewhat annoyed. But as these critical and (to Frank) arrogant remarks were made to millions of radio listeners he was completely enraged. He had Sammy fired from *Never So Few* and cut off all contact with him. Sinatra refused to listen if anyone mentioned his name. Peter Lawford tried to explain Sammy's side of things and Sinatra nearly flattened him. Sammy tried to speak to him on the telephone, but Sinatra wouldn't take his calls. When both were performing at hotels in Miami a few weeks later, Sinatra told the management of his establishment that Sammy was not even to be admitted in to see his show.

Sinatra only forgave Sammy after the latter went on another radio program and publicly apologized. This time,

Sinatra agreed to talk to Sammy on the phone. Sinatra came to accept that Sammy had never meant to be hurtful or cruel; he had simply let his honesty get carried away. Underneath all the misunderstandings and resentments, the two men genuinely liked each other, so they were easily able to patch up their friendship. It would be quite a few years before that friendship was again put to the test.

By this time the actor Humphrey Bogart, who'd once told Sammy's father and "Uncle" Will to retire from show business, had passed away from cancer. His original "rat pack" had disbanded. Sinatra had formed his own "Rat Pack," which included singer Dean Martin, comedian Joey Bishop, Peter Lawford, and of course, Sammy. Lawford came to Sinatra with a screenplay he had optioned entitled *Ocean's Eleven*. He thought it would be the perfect property for the entire rat pack to appear in.

Ocean's Eleven (1960) was about a man named Danny Ocean (Sinatra) who contacts several old paratrooper buddies whose lives have taken a bad turn since the service. Danny wants to enrich all of their coffers by pulling off one of the most daring heists of all time: robbing all the casinos in Las Vegas on the same night! Although Sammy was third-billed after Sinatra and Dean

Martin, his role of sanitation truck driver Josh Howard was rather small. In fact, it was not much bigger than the jeep driver in *Never So Few,* though his rendition of the title song adds a certain bluesy ambience to the picture. At least he received a hefty amount of money for his participation.

Ocean's Eleven received a mixed critical reaction. It was generally agreed that the funniest bit was the ending: the boys successfully pull off the robberies, but make the mistake of hiding the loot in a coffin — which is cremated along with the body inside it the next day! Their ill-gotten gains go up in ashes. The film was remade with an all new cast in 2002.

While they were filming the movie on location in Las Vegas, the boys stayed at the Sands Hotel; then they would perform in the hotel's Copa room each night. This meant that filming on *Ocean's Eleven* would rarely begin before noontime. When word got out that the famous Rat Pack were in Las Vegas, there was not a vacant hotel room to be found in either the Sands or anywhere else. The Copa room was sold out each night as tourists by the thousands showed up to see the Rat Pack perform in person.

The fivesome took to the stage to sing numbers

separately and together, heckle each other good-naturedly, tell ribald jokes, and basically fool around to the amusement of themselves and their audience. There was a bar on stage so that they got as tanked as the members of the audience. Sammy dressed each night in the wildest outfits he could cobble together as opposed to the tux all the other fellows wore. Tight pants, capes, boas, anything and everything.

Sammy's clothing would not only garner laughs from the audience and provide his friends on stage with material for ribbing, but also helped him maintain a kind of independence. Some of the humor on stage was racial but it was never meant to be hurtful. Dean Martin would pick up the diminutive Sammy in his hands, hold him high, and say "I'd like to thank the NAACP (National Association for the Advancement of Colored People) for this award!" Sammy became the Chairman of the Life Membership Committee of the NAACP in 1966, and also headed the membership drive for the Los Angeles chapter of the group. He received the Springham Medal from the group in the sixties for "the highest or noblest achievement by an American Negro during the preceding years."

In the early sixties the members of the Rat Pack were considered the epitome of "cool." They stayed up late, did what they pleased, drank as much as they wanted, lived lives that seemed to consist of endless fun and pure pleasure — all the while making millions of dollars. They put together their own language, slang words that were to be used only by the "in crowd." For instance, a "clyde" was a loser, a bore or a geek; "The Big Casino" referred to death; and "a little hey hey" was a good time or a sexual experience.

By the time Sinatra's Rat Pack had officially formed, Peter Lawford had married Pat Kennedy, whose brother was John Fitzgerald Kennedy. Lawford introduced Sinatra to Kennedy, and the two found they had much in common. When JFK decided to run for President, Sinatra made up his mind that his Rat Pack would help him campaign. He rechristened the Rat Pack the "Jack Pack" and made it clear that everyone's participation was mandatory. Sammy liked Kennedy's liberal attitudes on civil rights, so he had no problem stumping for him. For his part, Kennedy was glad to have the entire Rat Pack, Sammy included, on his side. Sadly, Sammy's race was to eventually become an issue.

For one thing, Sammy had fallen in love with a white woman. Her name was Mai (later May) Britt, and she was a Swedish actress who'd appeared in *The Young Lions*

The fabulous "Rat Pack"— from left: Frank Sinatra, Dean Martin, Sammy, actor Peter Lawford and comedian Joey Bishop—during their heyday in Las Vegas.

(1958) with Dean Martin and in other films. She was being groomed for stardom by Twentieth Century-Fox, but her career was never very important to her. She was introduced to Sammy at the studio commissary, and initially found him a little overbearing. Mai was somewhat shy and reserved and needed time to acclimate herself to

In the movie *Ocean's Eleven,* Sammy played a garbageman who collects the loot after his old army buddies have robbed five Las Vegas casinos.

new people and surroundings. Sammy's outgoing nature was a little overwhelming to Mai. Eventually he wore her down and she agreed to go out with him.

Although Sammy was initially attracted by Mai's good looks, she became much more than a beautiful blond trophy to him. Mai was afraid, however, that that was just how Sammy saw her: a sexy trophy that he could show off in front of friends and family. He made too many comments on her clothing; he was always suggesting she put on something sexier. She had heard that Sammy had been secretly dating blonde bombshell and movie star Kim Novak, and was afraid that she was only a substitute "goddess."

To test how serious he was about the relationship, Mai asked Sammy to fly to Sweden to meet her family. Sammy readily agreed. As far as he was concerned, this was the real deal, true love, and Mai was the only woman in the world for him. Mai came to feel the same way about Sammy: he was her soulmate. They were married on November 13th, 1960.

The marriage was supposed to have taken place several weeks earlier, but there were complications. For one thing, as soon as Mai and Sammy announced their engagement, they started receiving hate mail. In England, where Sammy flew for some club engagements, the outcry was much more limited. In his own country, however, it seemed every racist had crawled out from under a rock to make Sammy their personal whipping boy. Newspaper columnists, professing to be liberal, asked if a biracial union would be in the best interests of the subsequent children. "My kids will be 'black' in the eyes of the world whether their mother is white or black," countered Sammy.

There were those in the Kennedy camp who suggested it could hurt the campaign if Sinatra showed up at Sammy's wedding. There were ugly incidents at the Democratic National Convention in July; Sammy was booed and called racist names after the Rat Pack sang *The Star Spangled Banner*. This might have happened in any case, but it was certainly intensified by the news of his engagement to a white woman. While the heckling was limited to delegates from Mississippi, Sammy was so disheartened that he left the convention center almost in tears.

Frank, whose commitment to civil rights had never wavered, told Sammy that he was coming to the wedding with bells on, no matter what. Sammy was deeply touched by this gesture, but he insisted on postponing the wedding until after the election. Dismayed as he was by the entire unfair situation, Frank considered this an act of friendship above and beyond the call of duty. Sick as they were about the whole business, both men agreed that it was paramount to get Kennedy elected, as he was the best man to bring into effect the social changes they both desired.

Whatever loyalty Sinatra and Sammy had for each other, and for John Kennedy, that loyalty did not work in reverse — at least not as far as JFK was concerned. Once he was elected, Kennedy had his personal secretary call Sammy and tell him that he would prefer it if he did not attend his inauguration. The secretary put it oh so delicately — "your being there at this time may ultimately undermine the efforts Kennedy plans on behalf of civil rights; we hope you understand" and so forth — but it was still devastating to Sammy.

Sammy knew he probably would have been allowed to attend had he not married Mai, but if a black man wasn't free to marry anyone he chose, of any race, then was he really free at all? It was one of the worst humiliations he'd ever endured. Frank and the other Rat Packers would be there, but not the "nigger." He had come so far, but not far enough. He was gratified to learn that JFK's brother, Bobby, who would become Attorney General, had fought bitterly to have Sammy at the inauguration. In fact, Bobby would rather have cut ties with Sinatra, whose alleged mafia connections made him nervous.

Sinatra did not find out about this dreadful slight to Sammy until later, after he had organized some spectacular entertainment for the gala event. Later on, when he had served his purpose, Frank was also brushed off by the Kennedy camp because of his friendships with certain well-known gangsters. Both Sammy and Frank eventually campaigned for a Republican candidate, Richard Nixon, because they felt his commitment to civil rights was more genuine. Otherwise, Sammy was through with politics — and politicians.

Sammy continued to make movies during this period. He appeared in *Sergeants 3* (1962) with his fellow Rat Packers; this was an update of Rudyard Kipling's "*Gunga Din*." Sammy was cast in the Gunga Din role, although now he was a freed black slave named Jonah Williams. The picture did okay at the box office but was not admired by critics. "A 4 million dollar home movie for the gnat pack," opined *Time* magazine. Out of the cast, Sammy garnered the best reviews because he played with conviction while the others acted as if they'd rather be off playing golf.

That same year Sammy appeared in *Reprieve,* which was retitled *Convicts 4* to make it sound like a Rat Pack movie, which it wasn't. Instead of Frank and Dino, Sammy's co-stars were Vincent Price, Rod Steiger, and Stuart Whitman. Ben Gazzara starred as a prison inmate who learns how to paint during his lengthy time in stir. Sammy had a small role as a fellow prisoner.

By this time Sinatra had been set adrift by the Kennedys, for which he unfairly blamed JFK's brother-in-law Peter Lawford. Lawford was cut out of what was supposed to be the next Rat Pack movie, "4 for Texas"(1963); there were also no roles for Joey Bishop or Sammy. Part of the reason for this was that both men had agreed to appear in a film that Lawford was producing entitled *Johnny Cool* (1963). Sammy and Bishop had minor roles in this story of a psychotic gangster played by Henry Silva.

Sammy also appeared in a German film version of Kurt Weill's famous musical *The Three Penny Opera* (1963). In this he played the narrator, who comments on the action and characters, and sings *Mack the Knife*. Sammy not only fits into the mood of the piece very nicely and winningly, and sings well, but he easily steals the picture from everyone else in the cast. Displaying his enormous charisma and talent, he is the best thing about an otherwise dull and underproduced movie. The nominal stars were Curt Jurgens, Gert Frobe, and Hildegarde Knef, all of whom would eventually appear in American movies. (Jurgens and Frobe both wound up playing villains in James Bond movies, *The Spy Who Loved Me* and *Goldfinger,* respectively.)

Recent events had shown Sammy that while he might have come quite a distance in his life and career, black people (the term "African-American" was not in vogue at this time) still had quite a ways to go in America. He had always regretted that his first musical *Mr. Wonderful* had chickened out and watered down its message of black pride and equality.

That would not be the case with his next Broadway musical, *Golden Boy.*

Chapter Six

Golden Boy

Throughout the early sixties, Sammy continued his association with Frank Sinatra. Although Lawford was definitely out of the Pack by now, Sammy was included in another Rat Pack film entitled *Robin and the 7 Hoods* (1964). What would have been Lawford's part was taken by crooner Bing Crosby. Loosely based on the legend of Robin Hood, *Robin and the 7 Hoods* presents Robin (Sinatra) as a literal hood who gives money to orphanages and is embroiled in conflicts with other gangsters. A parody of crime melodramas of an earlier era, the movie took place in Chicago in the 1920's and the emphasis was on laughs and musical numbers.

Sammy was again third-billed and well-paid for his efforts, but it was easy to notice that again his role was almost a bit part. Any minor character actor or extra could have said the few lines he was given as one of the gang. He did get to sing a few bars, but it was only briefly in one of Bing Crosby's numbers, "Don't mess with Mr. Booze." Sammy plays a petty thief being "saved" by Crosby. Sinatra may have forgiven Sammy for those long-ago radio comments, but he didn't like the way he continued to associate with Peter Lawford, who Frank now actively hated. Sammy may have been grateful to Frank, but he himself had no quarrel with Lawford, who he liked; he thought Frank was all wrong to take out his anger at the Kennedys on Peter just because he had married into that family. Just as Lawford had once gone to bat for Sammy during the Jack Eigen debacle, Sammy tried to patch things up between Frank and Lawford, but it was no use. Then JFK was assassinated during the filming of *Robin and the 7 Hoods*, shutting down production for awhile. Jack Kennedy's death — even Pat Kennedy's divorcing Lawford in 1966 — didn't end the one-sided feud between Lawford and Sinatra.

Sammy had more important concerns, however. He was tapped to star in another Broadway show once shooting wrapped on *Robin and the 7 Hoods*. Working with Sinatra, he might always be in the Chairman's shadow, but on the stage, he could be top dog. The new musical, *Golden Boy*, had originally been a straight play by Clifford Odets; it premiered in 1937. Two years later it was turned into a movie starring William Holden and Barbara Stanwyck.

Odets had based his play on real-life prizefighter Mike Rubino, who had originally studied to be a violinist. After he almost lost the use of his arm due to an infection in a wound, he thought boxing would have therapeutic value. Instead it took over his life and became his new, highly-successful career. There was no reason why the main character of *Golden Boy* — a man who loves music but becomes a prizefighter to pay the bills — couldn't be turned into a black man. This was the part Sammy played.

Odets wrote the new book for the musical, but died before the show could come to Broadway. The first director, Peter Coe, was replaced in Boston by Arthur Penn (best-known for directing the film *Bonnie and Clyde*). When out-of-town tryouts made clear that the book needed revising, playwright William Gibson, most famous for *The Miracle Worker*, was brought in to make several changes. Lead character "Joe Bonaparte" became "Joe Wellington," and he was changed from an aspiring violinist to an aspiring surgeon who is afraid boxing might ruin his hands. In Odets' original play, Joe's brother was a union organizer; he was now turned into a civil rights leader.

After some more fine-tuning on the road, the show was set to open on Broadway in September of 1964. If they had stuck to that schedule, the show would have opened without Sammy Davis (who had dropped the "Jr." from his billing). Sammy was suffering from such exhaustion that he had to take two weeks off to recover. The opening was pushed back until October 20th. Although word on the street was that the show would be a disaster after so much drastic tinkering, it actually got mostly positive notices.

Unlike *Mr. Wonderful*, the new musical did absolutely nothing to take the audience's mind off the fact that the lead character was a black man. One number, the crowd-pleasing *Don't Forget 127th Street*, celebrated the "golden boy's" — and Sammy Davis Jr.'s — Harlem roots. The book for the musical not only had lines expressing the belief that Black was Beautiful, but poked gentle fun at white folks' misperceptions of blacks. During the aforementioned number when another black character starts to dance — badly — Sammy observes: "Now that I've seen you dance I am firmly convinced we ain't all born with it."

"I Can Do Anything"

The musical numbers by Adams and Strouse ("Bye, Bye, Birdie"; "It's a Bird, It's a Plane, It's Superman"; "Annie") were often an improvement on the songs in *Mr. Wonderful.* Sammy had plenty of opportunities to display his by now expert vocalizing. In "Night Song", in which his character sings about how he feels life is passing him by, Sammy interprets the song as well as Sinatra. He belts out "I Want to be With You" and "Can't You See It?" with aplomb. The line "tell me something's bad and I can't live without it" in the song "Gimme Some", which Sammy sang with young Johnny Brown, seemed to forecast Sammy's eventual problems with alcohol and drugs.

Two songs reflected the increasing militancy among blacks in the United States: "Colorful," in which Sammy sings of different colors and decides "black is best," and "No More," in which he vows that injustice against his people will no longer be tolerated. The most memorable number in the show, "While the City Sleeps" was a valentine to the night life and Bohemian lifestyle in New York City. The song was given to Billy Daniels, but Sammy could certainly relate to it. He was so tired and off his game when he made the original cast recording, that he re-recorded some of the songs during the show's run.

These are the ones that are used on the current CD of the show.

Others in the cast of *Golden Boy* included Paula Wayne as the girlfriend and, strangely, Ken Tobey, who'd appeared in such science fiction films as *The Thing from Another World,* and *The Beast from 20,000 Fathoms.* *Golden Boy* wracked up 569 performances, which made it a moderate hit. For his performance as Joe Wellington, the "*Golden Boy,*" Sammy was nominated for a Tony Award.

Golden Boy featured an interracial love story, but was actually not the first musical to do so. In the 1920's A racially-mixed woman briefly has a relationship with a white man in the aforementioned *Show Boat.* Rodgers and Hammerstein's *South Pacific* had featured a secondary romance between a white soldier and a beautiful Eurasian girl in the 1950's. In 1962, Richard Rodgers also wrote words and music (his partner Oscar Hammerstein having died) to *No Strings,* which, like *Golden Boy,* also featured a black/white romance, although with the sexes switched (white man romances black woman). Of the two shows *Golden Boy* was more daring, because to a mass audience in the sixties black women were more "acceptable" as lovers for Caucasian men than black men were for Caucasian women.

No Strings came off like pure fantasy, however. There were only oblique references made to race during the show, and stars Diahann Carroll and Richard Kiley never even embraced. Davis at least got to kiss his white girlfriend on stage in *Golden Boy*, though not full on the mouth or with any great passion. It may be that the interracial angle was worked into the storyline to capitalize on all the "publicity" over Sammy's own interracial marriage, or it may be that the producers felt there should be at least one major white character for the Caucasian members of the audience to identify with.

In addition to the musical, Sammy became a TV star with his own variety program, *The Sammy Davis Jr. Show*, on NBC. Prepping for the program and appearing on Broadway each night left him little time to carouse until all hours as he had done during the run of *Mr. Wonderful*. The program went through a number of title and format changes and emerged as *The Swinging World of Sammy Davis Jr.* in 1965. Both shows were nominated for Emmy Awards.

That same year Sammy had a small role in *Nightmare in the Sun*, a movie thriller starring Ursula Andress and husband John Derek. He also wrote his first autobiography, *Yes I Can,* which was named for a song that was dropped from *Golden Boy.*

Sammy's career was cooking, but his marriage wasn't doing as well. Wife May (by now she had changed the spelling of her name) had noticed how the wives of the other Rat Pack members seemed shunted aside and ignored while the "boys" went out to work (and play), and she swore it would not happen to her. But it had. She had given up her career to be a wife for Sammy, and now found herself alone too much of the time. Sammy would say he'd be right home after the show ended, but it wasn't long before he was staying out late with his friends. Worse, he would sometimes bring the whole gang back to his apartment. As May wanted some peace and quiet and time alone with her husband, the unwanted company was a blow to her morale.

Sammy would temporarily ease May's worries by telling her that things would change very soon. He told her that an entertainer had to go with the flow; when the big moment arrived you had to work harder than ever because every career had its inevitable downslide. A hit Broadway show, a TV series — now he was being tapped to *star* in a new movie. This was not the time for him to put the kibosh on his career by turning down any opportunity. Sure, the time they spent together was limited, but that would not always be the case. He gave May more spending money, a quick kiss, and was out the door before she knew what hit her.

The new movie was called *A Man Called Adam* (1966) and Sammy truly thought this was the major project he'd been waiting all his life for. It would, he felt, not only make him a superstar every bit as big as Frank, but also embody his personal philosophy even more than *Golden Boy* had. Sammy was brought into the film by his business manager, Jim Waters, who produced the film with Ike Jones — Jones became the very first black man to get a producing credit on a major American film release.

Nat King Cole was supposed to have played the title role of Adam Johnson, but he died before filming could begin. Adam was a trumpet player who is nearly dying of grief and guilt. While inebriated, he crashed up a car; his wife and child were killed in the accident, and his best friend lost his eyesight. (This angle resonated with Sammy, as he had almost lost his own eyesight in that terrible automobile accident.) A young woman feels sorry for Adam, and tries to help him get on with his life, which is complicated by the hatred felt for him by a racist agent.

On one hand Sammy was happy that the story could have been told about a man of any race — "Adam only happens to be a Negro," he told one interviewer. On the other hand, he ensured that script revisions would include many references to the plight of the Black Man in America. Many scenes that delineated character and provided a solid plot structure had to be excised to keep the running time at a manageable length. Sammy also insisted that Adam die at the end of the story. And he made Adam Johnson much more like Sammy Davis Jr. than he had been in the original script. Elements from his own life were incorporated into the screenplay.

Sammy had his first real starring part in *A Man Called Adam* — there was no Sinatra or Rat Pack, Dorothy Dandridge or Sidney Poitier to get in the way — and he was determined to make the movie as good as it possibly could be. In his determination, he may have gone overboard. To some, *A Man Called Adam* would be written off as an "ego trip." But Sammy really did want this project to not only showcase him at his best, but to say something meaningful to everyone who saw it. The troubles began, perhaps, when Sammy — influenced no doubt by friend Sinatra — practically took over the direction from the more experienced Leo Penn.

"I Can Do Anything"

At least Sammy surrounded himself with talented and sympathetic co-stars. Peter Lawford played the racist agent who bedevils him; Cecily Tyson was cast as the new lady friend who tries to help Adam. No less than Ossie Davis (no relation to Sammy) played his best friend who's blinded in the crash. Singer Mel Torme played himself in a nightclub scene, and the part of another young trumpet player went to Sinatra's son, Frank Sinatra Jr. Louis Armstrong also had a small role.

To increase the film's veracity, most of *A Man Called Adam* was shot on location in the streets of New York. The nightclub scenes were filmed at an actual Harlem club called Small's Paradise. When the film was released, most reviewers were kind but few were enthusiastic. The general consensus was that Sammy over-acted and that the film's script was too slight to make it a real contender; parts were better than the whole. Most critics recommended the movie only to Sammy's die-hard fans and serious jazz buffs. In only a year or two after its release *A Man Called Adam* was virtually forgotten.

By 1968, May Britt Davis had had enough of her marriage and Sammy's absences; she filed for divorce. May received custody of their three children: daughter Tracey, and two adopted sons, Mark and Jeff. The divorce was amicable, but probably a lot tougher on May than on Sammy, who had always been much more career-oriented. May at least had three children to give her love to, and that would have to be enough. Sammy had only so much to give. He gave so much — so much of his energy, experience and dedication — to his performing that there was very little left for his family. He loved May and the children, but entertaining was not only his livelihood but "his life".

Soon he was off to England for the London premiere of *Golden Boy* — and a comical misadventure or two with a former member of the Rat Pack.

Chapter Seven

One More Time

In 1968 Sammy and everyone else associated with *Golden Boy* figured the show, which had closed two years earlier, needed a second life. A new production of the show was fine-tuned in Chicago for several weeks, then headed for London, where it opened on June 4th and ran for 118 performances. Gloria DeHaven, who'd appeared in many films in the forties and fifties, now played Sammy's love interest. Generally the reviews were as good as they had been in New York. The show was sold to movie producer Joseph E. Levine, but a film adaptation never materialized. (There was a major off-Broadway revival of the show, with a new book and, of course, new stars, in 1984.)

The year before the London production of *Golden Boy*, Sammy and Peter Lawford had come to the same conclusion about their respective film careers: dead in the water. Sinatra wasn't sending any scripts Sammy's way. As these might have contained only minor parts for him (as the other Rat Pack movies had), Sammy wasn't too dismayed. Lawford was so washed up in Hollywood, partly due to nemesis Sinatra's behind-the-scenes machinations, that he turned to television for work. When these projects also dried up, Lawford was at his wit's end as to where to seek employment in show business. Sammy still had his club engagements and TV appearances, but he knew that the big money and superstar status came only by starring in major motion pictures, a la Sinatra.

Peter's friendship with Sammy never wavered, however. A chance remark by an acquaintance as to how he was "salt" and Sammy was "pepper," stuck in Lawford's mind. Salt and Pepper. It had a ring to it. Suppose they played characters with those last names in a movie. Only he, Peter, would be Pepper, and Sammy would be Salt. Peter thought he was on to something. Super-spies were all the rage during the sixties, and Dean Martin had had a big hit playing agent Matt Helm in a spy parody, *The Silencers* (1966) and its sequels. Maybe he and Sammy could play spies, too, in a funny movie that took advantage of their comic gifts.

The result was *Salt and Pepper* (1968), in which

Sammy in his "psychedelic" or "mod" phase in the 1960's. Here he appears in the movie *Sweet Charity*.

Sammy was Charlie Salt and Peter was Christopher Pepper. The two characters are co-owners of a discotheque who inadvertently become secret agents when several people are murdered in their establishment. Shanghaied to a Polaris submarine, they learn of a nefarious plot to overthrow Her Majesty's government. They manage to foil the would-be revolutionaries and are knighted for their services at the end of the picture.

Peter's own company, ChrisLaw, co-produced the film and hired both him and Sammy for $75,000 a piece. They decided to make the movie in London before *Golden Boy* opened and take advantage of the then in vogue obsession with all things British since the Beatles had invaded America. This was the era when everything "mod" (or trendily modern and hip) was in. Like men many years their junior, Sammy and Peter wore bellbottom pants, Nehru jackets, love beads, and bushy, over-sized sideburns – both on and off the screen.

The two men were fussed over by the British public as if they were Sinatra and Dean Martin, always considered the bigger stars. They rented suites at the stylish Mayfair Hotel, and ordered the best of everything — booze, caviar — for the lavish parties they threw virtually every night. They were desperately trying to recreate the "Rat Pack" magic at the Sands in Las Vegas during 1960.

Peter introduced Sammy to cocaine, the "happy dust" his character had sold in *Porgy and Bess*. It wasn't long before both developed expensive habits. Sammy took on London club engagements during filming so that he could afford his drugs. Dozens of willing women showed up at their suites to "audition" for roles in the film. One girl who simply moved in with Sammy and refused to leave nearly broke the duo up when she switched to Peter in mid-steam and had both men in a jealous tizzy. The matter was soon resolved, however, when they joined up to throw the girl out of the hotel.

Sammy and Peter managed to make a movie during this chaos, although director Richard Donner had his hands full. The two men rarely reported for filming before noon, and were usually hung over and in no condition to work. As they had trouble remembering the script, they improvised, but the new lines they came up with were only funny to themselves. Donner assumed he would be able to salvage the movie by cutting out the terrible ad libs in the editing room, but he was fired before he could do so.

When the studio objected to the rough cut assembled by Sammy and Peter themselves, they blamed Donner's inexperience as a director. Donner later went on to direct such films as *Superman* and *The Omen*. He swore he would never work with Davis or Lawford again.

Salt and Pepper did not impress many critics, but it proved popular with the public. Sammy gave his usual spirited performance, even if it was hardly calculated to garner any Oscar nominations. Lawford seemed to barely walk through the movie. *Salt and Pepper* surprised everyone by making so much money that it was decided to make a sequel. Besides, Sammy and Peter had spent so much of the production money on women, drugs, liquor and frequent parties at night clubs, that the profits from the film weren't as great as they might have hoped. Perhaps they could recoup their losses if the second *Salt and Pepper* movie were a hit.

Making the sequel would severely test the bonds of friendship between Sammy and Peter, however.

Sammy was featured in a big production number in the middle of the film adaptation of the Broadway show *Sweet Charity* (1969), in which he had the pleasure of working with old friend Shirley MacLaine. He had met Shirley during the heydays of the Rat Pack. Now and again she would pop up in his life to console or scold him, depending on the situation and her attitude. That same year he appeared in two minor films, *Gone with the West* and *Man without Mercy.*

The following year it was time to make the sequel to *Salt and Pepper*, which was called *One More Time*. One of the few people in Hollywood who had bucked Sinatra's edict and employed Peter Lawford was comedian Jerry Lewis, who cast him in *Hook, Line and Sinker.* Peter was grateful to Lewis and wanted to return the favor now that

Lewis' own career was on the wane. Sammy had been friends with Lewis for years and readily agreed that he should be hired to helm *One More Time*. For his part, Lewis considered Sammy to be "the singularly most talented one-man performer who ever lived."

Sammy and Peter rented a house in London where they partied as furiously as they did while shooting *Salt and Pepper*. Sammy was snorting more coke than ever. Somehow they managed to make it through the film, primarily because Lewis took such time setting up for each shot that they had plenty of time to relax before they were needed on camera. Lewis took the assignment very seriously, and nearly drove the film seriously over-budget by ordering special cameras and lenses, and even antique furniture for the settings. He was talked out of the last when reminded that some of this furniture would be destroyed in fight scenes and it would make more sense to use items from the prop department.

Once it was through, Jerry was allowed to edit the film on his own. Early in his career Jerry had been partnered with Rat Packer Dean Martin to form the comedy team Martin and Lewis. It seemed that he had done his best to turn *One More Time* into a kind of latter-day Martin and Lewis film with Sammy and Peter standing in for him and

Dino. Sammy was delighted with the results, but Lawford was mortified. The studio agreed and sided with Peter. Lewis was locked out of the editing room while his "masterpiece" was re-cut along more traditional lines. Sammy, siding with Jerry, was angry at Peter for not backing them up in their fight with the powers-that-be. Their relationship was never the same after that.

One More Time got the usual mixed reviews, but didn't do as well at the box office as the previous Salt and Pepper adventure. In this outing, Christopher Pepper takes the place of his twin brother to track down the dead man's killers. Of course, Charlie Salt is his partner in peril. The public seemed to have had enough of *Salt and Pepper* and Sammy and Peter had had enough of one another. There would be no more films together for them.

In 1970 Sammy married for the third and last time. His wife was an attractive black showgirl named Altovise Gore who had appeared in the London production of *Golden Boy*. Altovise had never really registered with Sammy when she was playing his sister on stage, but when he saw her all dolled up at a party the way she normally looked, his attention was riveted. For her part, Altovise was equally riveted by Sammy's boundless energy and the way he seemed to make her the center of his attention.

Altovise was as ambitious as Sammy, loved show business as much as he did, and also liked to party every bit as much as her husband. At first they seemed like the perfect match.

Sammy's children weren't so found of Altovise, and there were flare ups whenever they visited their father, especially between Altovise and Sammy's daughter, Tracey. Part of the problem was that Sammy was so busy when they visited that the children had to spend most of their time with Altovise, whom they barely knew. Tracey particularly resented it when Altovise, meaning well, tried to play mother. But she resented it much more when Sammy promised to show up for her high school graduation a few years later and never arrived.

By the time of his third marriage, Sammy's variety show was off the air, and he was chosen to star in a talk show called *Sammy and Company*. Sammy would chat with a guest and then do a number with them if they were singers or dancers; if not, Sammy would perform by himself. It was thought that his overall amiability — not to mention all of his show business contacts – would make him the perfect interviewer. The problem was that Sammy fawned so much over his famous guests that later even he described his manner as "sickening" and "cloying." The critics agreed and the show died quietly after only a few months.

On a brighter note, in 1971 Sammy had a cameo in the James Bond film *Diamonds are Forever*; he also appeared in the music documentary *Save the Children* in 1973. The latter movie was filmed at a concert held in Chicago for Operation PUSH (People United to Save Humanity), which was organized by Jesse Jackson.

Sammy had had twenty-two albums and sixteen singles released since his first LP in 1955. His advisers felt that his long-time record label, Reprise (he also did some albums for Decca early in his career), wasn't doing much to promote his recordings, so they suggested he hop to the number one company for black recording artists. This was the Detroit-based Motown records. At first the executives at Motown were delighted to have Sammy on board, but their attitude changed once his first album for them was released (on their Harmony imprint) and went nowhere.

The trouble was that fans of the Motown sound were generally young people of all races, and most of Sammy's fans at this point were middle-aged and older. Motown had no idea how to reach his target audience. Although they had made a second album with Sammy, Motown

declined to release it. Bitterly disappointed, Sammy
looked around for a new label.

In 1972 Sammy recorded "The Candy Man," written
by British song-writing team Anthony Newley and Leslie
Bricusse. This was his first record for his new label, MGM
records, after he was let out of his contract at Motown.
Although Sammy at first thought the song was a bit too
saccharine for his taste, he was delighted when it became
his biggest hit record of all time.

A charming number, "The Candy Man" features some
fine vocalizing from Sammy and is also well-produced and
handsomely arranged. It was originally written for a Walt
Disney picture, although many people who've heard the
record have mistakenly assumed the "candy man" is a drug
dealer. Sammy also recorded a second single, his last,
entitled "The People Tree", for MGM, but it did not do
nearly as well.

Over the years Sammy had become a much respected
vocalist. He was seen by music critics as a singer who
didn't just have a "pretty" voice, but one who could put
deep feeling into his interpretation of the lyrics. Sammy
sang so many different types of songs in so many styles
that it is generally considered that he failed to develop a
recognizable "identity." This kept him from garnering all

the acclaim that he was due.

Jazz enthusiasts feel his best recordings are the ones he did with orchestrator Marty Paich. When the jazz treatment is appropriate as in "Why Can't We Be Friends?", these recordings are wonderful. When inappropriate (Rodgers and Hart's "Falling in Love with Love" and indeed most show tunes), they fall completely flat. Sammy's finest recordings include "Gonna Build a Mountain", which is well-suited to his style; his saucy and sexy version of "Begin the Beguine"; his splendid, well-sung cover of "My Romance"; and "Lots of Livin' to Do", among others. A highly sophisticated vocalist, Sammy really knew how to *use* his voice.

Sammy got mostly strong notices for his one-man show *Sammy on Broadway*, which opened in 1974. His next Broadway venture was *Stop the World — I Want to Get Off* (1978), which had been a big hit in London for the aforementioned team of Newley and Bricusse a few years before. Sammy had already recorded songs from the show, including "What Kind of Fool Am I?" Although the number proved a bit of a strain for Sammy's voice, he otherwise gave a strong performance on another well-produced and arranged recording. One line, "I wasn't cut out to be husband or father.." resonated with Sammy.

Sammy became friends with Newley and his then wife, actress Joan Collins, and would often socialize with the couple. Collins remembered how Sammy would go around offering everyone coke.

It was undoubtedly the huge success of *Candy Man* that led Sammy to do his own version of the song-writing team's London musical. *Stop the World — I Want to Get Off* was an allegory about the adventures of a fellow named LittleChap, an average man or "everyman" coming up against life and its travails. Transplanted to America and with a change of lead from young Englishman to Sammy Davis Jr., most critics agreed that the show just didn't work. Although the musical had already been filmed in 1966 (an almost literal record of the show), Sammy did his own cinematic adaptation entitled *Sammy Stops the World* in 1979. This, if anything, was even more excoriated than the Broadway version. As one critic put it, "*Sammy Stops the World* combines nail-your-camera-to-the-ground direction with a stage production that couldn't get by at Three Mile Island Dinner Theater." Sammy would not talk much about the film in later years.

Luckily, there would be at least one more notable screen appearance for Sammy in the 1980's — and, unfortunately, trouble and heartbreak as well.

Chapter Eight

Tapped Out

Throughout the seventies, Sammy Davis continued to abuse his body by overindulging in alcohol and illegal drugs. He gave coke parties in his Hollywood home where he would pass out little silver spoons to his guests for them to dip into a snuff bowl he used to hold the drug. He developed a pot belly from all the liquor, and memory loss problems due to his addiction to cocaine. He would tell a joke while on stage and wonder why no one had laughed. He had no idea that only ten minutes earlier he had told the same joke.

In other words, Sammy Davis Jr. was in serious trouble. To make matters worse, the cocaine habit and high spending in general created huge financial difficulties. He owed millions in back taxes. When he was afraid how it would look if people thought he was broke, he and Altovise threw a $75,000 catered party which they could

Sammy in middle age with mustache and goatee.

not afford. Sammy was never fiscally responsible, and bought pretty things for himself and his wife instead of paying the IRS what he owed. Every time he managed to pay a large bill, he would celebrate by going out for an expensive dinner.

One time, when he was too drunk to continue his performance, Sammy picked up the tab for eight hundred people in the audience: $17,000! Before long, the IRS was threatening to seize his Beverly Hills home. This resulted in Sammy making arrangements to pay off the huge debts and a temporary bout of economizing at home.

By this time, Frank Sinatra was no longer talking to Sammy; this was the second major breach in their friendship. Sammy learned that Frank had found out about his drug use and was furious with him. Sammy and others thought it was hypocritical of Sinatra to judge Sammy on this, as it was well known how drunk and out of control Frank could get. Sammy loved Frank, but he didn't want anyone, especially Frank, telling him how to behave. But drinking alcohol was legal, Sinatra felt, and snorting cocaine was not. However much Frank drank, his career didn't suffer for it. But Sammy's heavy drug use was playing havoc with his stage routine.

Altovise and Frank's wife, Barbara, arranged to have the two men meet together for dinner. That night Frank reaffirmed how much he cared for Sammy, and told him he was terribly afraid that the drug addictions would ultimately take away everything he had struggled so hard for over the years. Sammy knew that Frank was right and made up his mind then and there to purge hard drugs from his system. He also gave up booze when his doctor told him he had developed serious liver damage and would die if he continued drinking. From then on, he would sip on Orange soda and nothing else.

Once these demons were dealt with, there was an equally serious problem to face. Sammy began to feel a great deal of pain when he was dancing. It was determined that he required surgery on his hip. It is possible that the problem had been worsening for some time but that the alcohol and cocaine had dulled the pain and prevented Sammy from realizing something was seriously wrong. He was terribly afraid that a hip replacement might adversely affect his dancing, but friends such as Shirley MacLaine reminded him that with the surgery at least there was a chance he could go on dancing. Without it, there was no chance at all.

Sammy had the surgery, but was so worried over the results that he was difficult to deal with during convalescence. For a long time he had to hobble around with a cane. The first stage show he did after the operation was the ultimate test of how much the audience liked Sammy Davis Jr. He couldn't dance, his voice was too hoarse to sing or do impressions, so all he could do was sit on stage and tell stories. What on earth would the people out there think of him? he wondered.

He told the audience about that time he'd picked up everyone's tab, but said he had no intention of doing that ever again. The audience roared with warm appreciation, and he had them in his hand. He eventually was able to chuck the cane and do some dancing again. Although his movements may have been comparatively limited, he was nevertheless remarkable for a man who was nearly sixty at the time.

Sammy did a new film in 1981 entitled *The Cannonball Run.* Director Hal Needham and stars Burt Reynolds and Dom DeLuise tried to create some rat pack magic and even went so far as to cast Sammy and Dean Martin. Unfortunately, they were a far cry from the real Rat Pack in their hey day. The movie had to do with a zany cross country race with wild cars and even wilder drivers. Sammy and Dino were cast as two competitors who dress up as priests; they figure they can break all the speed laws they want and the cops will think they're rushing to give someone the Last Rites.

While critics hated the movie, *The Cannonball Run* did surprisingly well at the box office, and *Cannonball Run II* appeared in 1983. The highlight of the sequel was when

Sammy, along with Burt and Dom, dressed up like a dame in a harem and the three lip-synced to a recording of the Supremes *Stop in the Name of Love*. Sammy and Dino reprised their roles from the first film, but in midstream exchanged their priest's robes for policemen's uniforms. Sinatra did a bit which he filmed in one take in one afternoon.

The movies were more fun to make than to watch. Like the superior Rat Pack films, the movies themselves were secondary to the laughs the actors had while they made them.

In 1989 Sammy appeared in a far more memorable vehicle, *Tap,* which starred Gregory Hines as a former dancer turned second story man. When he gets out of prison, his old buddies try to get him back into the crime game, but his girlfriend's father, Little Mo (Sammy), inspires him to get back into his dancing shoes and go after the success he deserves. A valentine to the grand old style of tap dancing (that has been replaced by a new "Broadway" style that is not the same as done by masters in the twenties and thirties), *Tap*'s highlight is a scene when Hines challenges the older men in a dance studio to show their "legs." This results in a wonderful dance contest that climaxes with Hines and Sammy — still exhibiting his fine form and charisma — squaring off against each other in a tap-dancing competition. (In tap dancing, the feet tap out a beat as they are moved very *rapidly* in place, even as the dancers themselves move about in all directions. It is almost as if the feet are independent of the body.)

While *Tap* is so old-fashioned in some ways that it seems like a film from another era, it was a far worthier project for Sammy than the *Cannonball* movies. He was sixty-four when he made the film, but (due to illness) looks much older. His performance as Little Mo is ingratiating and believable. Gregory Hines also did solid work, as did Suzzanne Douglas as Little Mo's daughter. The film was written and directed by Nick Castle, whose father (also Nick Castle) was a top choreographer. *Tap* proved to be Sammy's final screen appearance.

After filming *Tap* (and before the film was released), Sammy re-teamed with Dean Martin and Frank Sinatra for what came to be known alternately as the *Together Again, Rat Pack*, and finally *Ultimate* Tour. Sammy and Frank both missed the excitement of the Rat Pack days in Las Vegas, and also wanted to bring Dean out of the dumps he'd been in since the tragic death of his son in a plane crash. Instead of entertaining in smoky intimate

Sammy was ill and looked older than his years while he made
his final movie *Tap*.

lounges, the boys hoped to fill whole stadiums, which they did not always do. Frank, however, liked the idea of more people seeing them in this one tour than all the people who'd seen them in Las Vegas over the years put together.

Martin did not particularly want to do the tour, and after some friction with Frank, left early. Sammy and Frank carried on alone for awhile, then brought in Liza Minelli for European engagements. Sammy greatly enjoyed the excitement of the tour and of performing with his buddies again, but he felt utterly exhausted more often than not. When he got back home he consulted his doctor.

The news was not good. Sammy had throat cancer. After a regimen of chemotherapy that left him feeling completely depleted, the cancer went into remission for awhile. But soon it came back more devastating than ever. Sammy was admitted to Cedars-Sinai Hospital for a spell, but when it became clear that his condition was terminal, his family importuned him to stay at home in Beverly Hills where everything would be done to make him as comfortable as possible. Private nurses looked after his needs, and he was hooked up to assorted monitors and tubes. There was a tense truce between daughter Tracey and wife Altovise, who still did not get along.

Among many others, Frank Sinatra came to see him

on a regular basis. Although Sammy was cheered by these visits from his old and dear friend, Sinatra was thoroughly disheartened to see Sammy, once an irrepressible ball of energy, just wasting away. He would climb down the stairs from Sammy's bedroom and barely be able to speak to anyone.

One bright note was that Sammy's daughter Tracey was married by this time and presented him with his first grandchild, a boy, before he died. It was almost as if a new life had come into the world to replace the old one that was leaving it. Another bright note was a phone call from President George Bush (Sr.) and his wife, Barbara, although Sammy was too ill at the time to take it. Instead the Bushes sent their best wishes through Altovise. The call came not a moment too soon. Sammy Davis Jr. died on May 16th, 1990 at the age of sixty-four.

✳

At a tribute to Davis that was held a few weeks before his death, such black entertainers as Gregory Hines, Eddie Murphy, Bill Cosby, Stevie Wonder, Whitney Houston, and Michael Jackson, expressed their admiration to Davis and the debt they owed him. As Jackson put it, "Thanks to you there's now a door we all walk through; I am here 'cause you were there."

President Bush issued a statement through his press secretary: "Mr. Davis has been a major figure in the entertainment world. His legacy of humor and songs, as well as charity work, will continue to be a part of future generations. The President and Mrs. Bush extend their sympathy and condolences to Mr. Davis' family and friends."

In addition to the honors already mentioned, Davis was cited by the League of Crippled Children and the Police Association of American for his work on their behalf, and also received a Kennedy Center Award for career achievement. In 1974 he was knighted by the Ecumenical Knights of Malta for "bringing happiness to untold millions of people throughout the world."

Sammy left an estate that was valued at about four million dollars. Two years after his death, the IRS was still trying to collect the back taxes he owed from his estate. In May 1997, the IRS and Sammy's widow, Altovise Davis, finally came to an undisclosed settlement which wrote *finis* to the seven million dollar liability. "I know he would have wanted us to reach a settlement with the government rather than declare bankruptcy," said Altovise at the time.

"He loved this country and the people in it and recognized his responsibilities as an American."

Three years later, in September of 2000, small items in several papers noted the passing of Elvera Sanchez Davis, Sammy Davis' mother, who died at age ninety-five, living ten years longer than her son. She had been involved with the world of tap-dancing for many, many years, even serving as an advisor to the New York Committee to Celebrate National Tap Dance Day from 1989 until her death. She was survived by a daughter, Ramona, Sammy's half-sister. Sammy had had little to do with them during his life.

Perhaps because it had been *his father* — and "Uncle Will" — who'd turned him into Sammy Davis, Jr., *superstar*.

Bibliography

Davis Jr., Sammy, and Jane and Burt Boyar. *"Sammy"*: an autobiography with material newly revised from *Yes I Can* and *Why Me?*. New York: Farrar, Strauss and Giroux; 2000.

Davis, Tracey, with Delores A. Barclay. *Sammy Davis Jr. — My Father*. Los Angeles: General Publishing Group; 1996.

Friedwald, Will. *Jazz Singing*. New York: Collier Books; 1992.

Quirk, Lawrence J. *The Kennedys in Hollywood*. Dallas: Taylor Publishing; 1996.

_____ and William Schoell. *The Rat Pack: Neon Nights with the Kings of Cool.*. New York: Avon; 1998.

Schoell, William. *Martini Man: The Life of Dean Martin*. Dallas:Taylor Publishing; 1999.

_____ *Heartbreaker: The Dorothy Dandridge Story.* Greensboro: Avisson Press; 2002.

Also consulted were articles and reviews *in Variety, The New York Times, The New York Daily and Sunday News, The New York Post Ebony, Jet, U.S. News and World Report; Library Journal; Hollywood Reporter,* and other periodicals and public documents.

Index

About the Author

WILLIAM SCHOELL, an expert on the members of the Rat Pack, including Sammy Davis Jr. (whom he terms "the most talented member of the pack") has talked about them on such TV shows as *Inside Edition, American Journal, and Hard Copy*, among others, as well as on numerous radio programs and lecture series. He has written books on Sinatra and the Rat Pack, Dean Martin, and now, Sammy Davis Jr. He has also written well-received biographies (for both adults and young adults) of Steven Spielberg, Joan Crawford, Al Pacino, Jules Verne, and H. P. Lovecraft, among others.